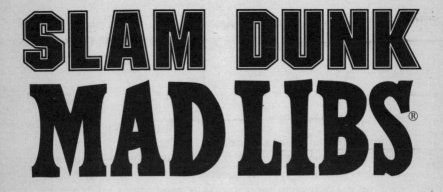

SLAM DUNK MAD LIBS

By Roger Price and Leonard Stern

PRICE STERN SLOAN
Los Angeles

ISBN: 0-8431-3722-3

10 9 8 7 6 5 4 3 2 1

MAD LIBS®

MAD LIBS® is a game for people who don't like games. It can be played by two, three, four, or forty.

■ RIDICULOUSLY SIMPLE DIRECTIONS

In this tablet you will find stories containing blank spaces where words are left out. One player, the **READER**, selects one of these stories. The **READER** does not tell anyone what the story is about. Instead he/she asks the other players, the **WRITERS**, to give him/her words. These words are used to fill in the blank spaces in the story.

■ TO PLAY

The **READER** asks each **WRITER** in turn to call out a word. This word will be an adjective or a noun or whatever the space calls for. He/She then writes the words in the blank spaces in the story. After all the spaces are filled in, the result is a **MAD LIB**.

The **READER** then reads the completed **MAD LIB** to the other players. They will hear that they have written a story that is fantastic, screamingly funny, shocking, silly, crazy, or just plain dumb—depending upon which words each **WRITER** called out.

In case you've forgotten what adjectives, adverbs, nouns, and verbs are, here is a quick review:

An **ADJECTIVE** describes something or somebody. *Lumpy, soft, ugly, messy,* and *short* are adjectives.

An **ADVERB** tells how something is done. It modifies a verb and usually ends in "ly." *Modestly, stupidly, greedily,* and *carefully* are adverbs.

A **NOUN** is the name of a person, place or thing. *Sidewalk, umbrella, bridle, bathtub,* and *nose* are nouns.

A **VERB** is an action word. *Run, pitch, jump,* and *swim* are verbs.

When we ask for a **GEOGRAPHICAL LOCATION**, we mean any sort of place: a country or city (Spain, Cleveland) or a room (bathroom, kitchen).

An **EXCLAMATION** or **SILLY WORD** is any sort of funny sound, gasp, grunt or outcry. *Wow! Ouch! Whomp! Ick! Gadzooks!* are exclamations and silly words.

When we ask for specific words like **A NUMBER, A COLOR, AN ANIMAL,** or **A PART OF THE BODY**, we mean a word that is one of those things.

When a **PLURAL** is asked for, be sure to pluralize the word. For example, *cat* pluralized is *cats*.

EXAMPLE: _____

(BEFORE)

" _____ !" he said

EXCLAMATION

_____ , as he jumped into his

ADVERB

convertible_____and drove off

NOUN

with his _____ wife.

ADJECTIVE

(AFTER)

" *Ouch!* _____ !" he said

EXCLAMATION

Stupidly _____ , as he jumped into his

ADVERB

convertible *Stomach* _____and drove off

NOUN

with his *brave* _____ wife.

ADJECTIVE

MAD LIBS® is fun to play with friends, but you can also play it by yourself! To begin with, DO NOT look at the story on the page below. Fill in the blanks on this page with the words called for. Then, using the words you've selected, fill in the blank spaces in the story.

Now you've created your own hilarious MAD LIB!

BASKETBALL PLAYOFFS

NAME OF PERSON IN ROOM: _____

NOUN: _____

ADJECTIVE: _____

VERB (PAST TENSE): _____

PLURAL NOUN: _____

PLURAL NOUN: _____

NUMBER: _____

ADJECTIVE: _____

ADJECTIVE: _____

NOUN: _____

EXCLAMATION: _____

NOUN: _____

NAME OF PERSON IN ROOM: _____

NOUN: _____

NOUN: _____

NUMBER: _____

NOUN: _____

NOUN: _____

NOUN: _____

BASKETBALL PLAYOFFS
(To be read enthusiastically)

Hi! This is _____ speaking to you
　　　　　　NAME OF PERSON IN ROOM

from the broadcasting_____at the_____
　　　　　　　　　　　NOUN　　　　　　　　　ADJECTIVE

forum. In case you_____in late, the score
　　　　　　　　　VERB (PAST TENSE)

between the Los Angeles_____and the Boston
　　　　　　　　　　　　　PLURAL NOUN

_____ is a squeaker, 141 to _____ .
　　PLURAL NOUN　　　　　　　　　　　　　　　NUMBER

This has been the most _____ game these
　　　　　　　　　　　　　　ADJECTIVE

_____eyes have seen in years. First one team scores
　　　ADJECTIVE

a _____ , then _____ !
　　　NOUN　　　　　　　　　　EXCLAMATION

the other team comes right back. Okay. Time-out is over. Los Angeles

brings in the ball at mid- _____ .
　　　　　　　　　　　　　　　　NOUN

_____ dribbles down the
　　　NAME OF PERSON IN ROOM

_____, fakes the defender out of his_____
　　　NOUN　　　　　　　　　　　　　　　　　　　　　NOUN

and shoots a _____ handed shot. It goes right through
　　　　　　　　　NUMBER

the_____. He beat the_____! The game
　　　NOUN　　　　　　　　　　　NOUN

is over just as the_____ goes off.
　　　　　　　　　　　NOUN

MAD LIBS® is fun to play with friends, but you can also play it by yourself! To begin with, DO NOT look at the story on the page below. Fill in the blanks on this page with the words called for. Then, using the words you've selected, fill in the blank spaces in the story.

Now you've created your own hilarious MAD LIB!

STRIKE 3, YOU'RE OUT!

NOUN: _____

NOUN: _____

NOUN: _____

ADJECTIVE: _____

NOUN: _____

NOUN: _____

NOUN: _____

ADJECTIVE: _____

NOUN: _____

NOUN: _____

NOUN: _____

NOUN: _____

NOUN: _____

NOUN: _____

ADJECTIVE: _____

ANIMAL (PLURAL): _____

STRIKE 3, YOU'RE OUT!

If you are sitting in a ball _____ and you hear fans
                                    NOUN

yelling "Get rid of the _____!" you know they mean the
                              NOUN

_____. An umpire is easy to recognize. He generally
       NOUN

wears a/an _____ suit and has a large padded
                 ADJECTIVE

_____ to protect his _____. At all games,
       NOUN   NOUN

there are four umpires—one at home _____, one at
                                              NOUN

first base, one at second base, and the other at

_____ base. The home plate umpire crouches
       ADJECTIVE

behind the _____ and decides whether the pitch is a
                 NOUN

ball or a/an _____. The umpires in the field decide if a
                  NOUN

player has stolen a/an _____, beat out a/an
                              NOUN

_____ or whether a fly ball is _____ or
       NOUN   NOUN

foul. An umpire may throw players out of the _____
                                                    NOUN

for calling them _____ names or saying they
                        ADJECTIVE

are as blind as _____.
                    ANIMAL (PLURAL)

MAD LIBS® is fun to play with friends, but you can also play it by yourself! To begin with, DO NOT look at the story on the page below. Fill in the blanks on this page with the words called for. Then, using the words you've selected, fill in the blank spaces in the story.

Now you've created your own hilarious MAD LIB!

HOW TO SERVE A TENNIS BALL ... OR EVEN LUNCH

ADJECTIVE: _____

NOUN: _____

NOUN: _____

ADVERB: _____

PART OF BODY: _____

PART OF BODY (PLURAL): _____

NOUN: _____

NOUN: _____

ADJECTIVE: _____

ADJECTIVE: _____

PART OF BODY: _____

NOUN: _____

NOUN: _____

ADJECTIVE: _____

NOUN: _____

HOW TO SERVE A TENNIS BALL...OR EVEN LUNCH

Here are some _____ suggestions to help improve
              ADJECTIVE

your tennis_____.
        NOUN

1. As you bounce your_____, imagine where you want it
              NOUN

   to land. Keep this image _____ in your
                        ADVERB

   _____.
       PART OF BODY

2. By bending your _____, you are
              PART OF BODY (PLURAL)

   able to push off the _____ and put more of your
                  NOUN

   _____ into your _____ serve.
      NOUN   ADJECTIVE

3. Remember, if you have relaxed and _____
                            ADJECTIVE

   muscles, you can let your _____ snap like
                     PART OF BODY

   a/an _____ and serve a/an _____.
         NOUN   NOUN

If you follow this_____ advice, in no time you
                 ADJECTIVE

can be a Wimbledon _____.
             NOUN

MAD LIBS® is fun to play with friends, but you can also play it by yourself! To begin with, DO NOT look at the story on the page below. Fill in the blanks on this page with the words called for. Then, using the words you've selected, fill in the blank spaces in the story.

Now you've created your own hilarious MAD LIB!

SWIMMING

PLURAL NOUN: _____

ADJECTIVE: _____

VERB (PRESENT TENSE): _____

NOUN: _____

PART OF BODY: _____

PART OF BODY(PLURAL): _____

VERB (PRESENT TENSE): _____

ADJECTIVE: _____

ADJECTIVE: _____

VERB (PRESENT TENSE): _____

ADJECTIVE: _____

NOUN: _____

NOUN: _____

SWIMMING

Many Americans have swimming _____ in their
                                PLURAL NOUN

backyards and learn to swim at a very_____age.
                                        ADJECTIVE

Learning   to   swim   is   easier   than   learning   to

_____ or to read a/an _____.
VERB (PRESENT TENSE)   NOUN

First you float on your_____, then you practice
                            PART OF BODY

kicking your _____ until you're able
                    PART OF BODY (PLURAL)

to _____ across the pool. If you work
        VERB (PRESENT TENSE)

hard, in no time at all you can master the_____
                                                ADJECTIVE

crawl, the _____ stroke and you can even
                ADJECTIVE

_____ underwater. Remember, with
VERB (PRESENT TENSE)

lots of practice you can become a/an _____
                                            ADJECTIVE

champion _____ on the U.S. Olympic
                NOUN

_____.
NOUN

MAD LIBS® is fun to play with friends, but you can also play it by yourself! To begin with, DO NOT look at the story on the page below. Fill in the blanks on this page with the words called for. Then, using the words you've selected, fill in the blank spaces in the story.

Now you've created your own hilarious MAD LIB!

ANOTHER DAY, ANOTHER MILLION

PLURAL NOUN: _____

NOUN: _____

NOUN: _____

NAME OF PERSON IN ROOM: _____

NOUN: _____

ADJECTIVE: _____

ADJECTIVE: _____

NOUN: _____

ADJECTIVE: _____

EXCLAMATION: _____

PART OF BODY: _____

ADJECTIVE: _____

PLURAL NOUN: _____

VERB (ENDING IN "ING"): _____

NOUN: _____

ANOTHER DAY, ANOTHER MILLION

Today the Chicago _____ announced the signing
PLURAL NOUN

of their number-one draft _____ to a million dollar
NOUN

_____. _____ was the
NOUN   NAME OF PERSON IN ROOM

highest scoring _____ ever to play for a/an
NOUN

_____ basketball team. In a/an
ADJECTIVE

_____ interview at his parents' _____
ADJECTIVE   NOUN

this morning, America's most recent _____ millionaire
ADJECTIVE

has this to say, " _____! I only hope I can keep
EXCLAMATION

my _____ screwed on straight." He threw his
PART OF BODY

_____ arms around his folks'
ADJECTIVE

_____, nearly _____
PLURAL NOUN   VERB (ENDING IN "ING")

the _____ out of them.
NOUN

From *SLAM DUNK MAD LIBS* ® ● Copyright © 1994 by Price Stern Sloan, Inc.

A member of The Putnam & Grosset Group, New York, New York.

MAD LIBS® is fun to play with friends, but you can also play it by yourself! To begin with, DO NOT look at the story on the page below. Fill in the blanks on this page with the words called for. Then, using the words you've selected, fill in the blank spaces in the story.

Now you've created your own hilarious MAD LIB!

THE COMEBACK KID

NAME OF PERSON IN ROOM: _____

ADVERB: _____

PLURAL NOUN: _____

PLURAL NOUN: _____

PLURAL NOUN: _____

NUMBER: _____

NUMBER: _____

NOUN: _____

PART OF BODY: _____

A LIQUID: _____

REPEAT NAME OF PERSON IN ROOM: _____

ADJECTIVE: _____

PLURAL NOUN: _____

NOUN: _____

PLURAL NOUN: _____

NOUN: _____

NUMBER: _____

NOUN: _____

THE COMEBACK KID

" _____ is back!" That's what
NAME OF PERSON IN ROOM

thousands of _____ fans kept shouting at the top
ADVERB

of their _____ as the San Francisco
PLURAL NOUN

_____ defeated the Miami _____
PLURAL NOUN   PLURAL NOUN

_____ to _____. After almost two years of sitting on the
NUMBER   NUMBER

_____ with his broken _____
NOUN   PART OF BODY

in a bucket of _____ , football great
A LIQUID

_____ returned to the game
REPEAT NAME OF PERSON IN ROOM

and led his team to a/an _____ victory. In addition
ADJECTIVE

to running for two _____ and throwing a/an
PLURAL NOUN

_____-breaking twelve _____
NOUN   PLURAL NOUN

in a row, he saved the game by recovering a/an _____
NOUN

on the _____ yard _____.
NUMBER   NOUN

MAD LIBS® is fun to play with friends, but you can also play it by yourself! To begin with, DO NOT look at the story on the page below. Fill in the blanks on this page with the words called for. Then, using the words you've selected, fill in the blank spaces in the story.

Now you've created your own hilarious MAD LIB!

FISHING

NOUN: _____

ADJECTIVE: _____

VERB (PRESENT TENSE): _____

NOUN: _____

ADVERB: _____

ADJECTIVE: _____

NOUN: _____

NOUN: _____

ADJECTIVE: _____

NOUN: _____

NOUN: _____

A LIQUID: _____

NOUN: _____

ADJECTIVE: _____

NOUN: _____

ADJECTIVE: _____

NOUN: _____

FISHING

Fishing is simple. All you need is a fishing _____ and
NOUN

a can of _____ worms. It's easy to tell when you
ADJECTIVE

_____ a fish. Your float will bob up and
VERB (PRESENT TENSE)

down or your _____ will unwind _____.
NOUN   ADVERB

If you want to catch bass, _____ trout or
ADJECTIVE

wall-eyed _____, you fish in a lake or a mountain
NOUN

_____. If it's _____ fin tuna you're
NOUN   ADJECTIVE

after or a sail- _____ or a sword- _____,
NOUN   NOUN

you go deep _____ fishing. This can be expensive.
A LIQUID

You may have to charter a/an _____ with a captain
NOUN

and a/an _____ mate to sail the _____.
ADJECTIVE   NOUN

Warning! The sea can be very _____ and you
ADJECTIVE

could become _____ sick.
NOUN

MAD LIBS® is fun to play with friends, but you can also play it by yourself! To begin with, DO NOT look at the story on the page below. Fill in the blanks on this page with the words called for. Then, using the words you've selected, fill in the blank spaces in the story.

Now you've created your own hilarious MAD LIB!

THE ROAR OF THE CROWD

PLURAL NOUN: _____

ADJECTIVE: _____

PLURAL NOUN: _____

ADJECTIVE: _____

NOUN: _____

ADJECTIVE: _____

ADJECTIVE: _____

PLURAL NOUN: _____

PLURAL NOUN: _____

PLURAL NOUN: _____

NOUN: _____

PLURAL NOUN: _____

PART OF BODY (PLURAL): _____

NOUN: _____

THE ROAR OF THE CROWD

It used to be that fans just stood up in their _____

                                        PLURAL NOUN

and yelled _____ words to their team. Today all

              ADJECTIVE

universities and even professional _____ have

                                PLURAL NOUN

cheerleaders. The male cheerleaders wear pants and

_____ sweaters with their school

             ADJECTIVE

_____ written across them. Female cheerleaders wear

   NOUN

_____ sweaters, _____ skirts

     ADJECTIVE   ADJECTIVE

and on their bare _____, _____

                PLURAL NOUN   PLURAL NOUN

and sneakers.

Before the game starts, the cheerleaders run onto the field shaking

their pom- _____ and turning _____

          PLURAL NOUN   NOUN

wheels. Then they hold _____ to their

                           PLURAL NOUN

_____ and stir the crowd into a frenzy

   PART OF BODY (PLURAL)

by yelling "Yeah! _____!"

               NOUN

From *SLAM DUNK MAD LIBS* ® ● Copyright © 1994 by Price Stern Sloan, Inc.
A member of The Putnam & Grosset Group, New York, New York.

MAD LIBS® is fun to play with friends, but you can also play it by yourself! To begin with, DO NOT look at the story on the page below. Fill in the blanks on this page with the words called for. Then, using the words you've selected, fill in the blank spaces in the story.

Now you've created your own hilarious MAD LIB!

BOWLING

ADJECTIVE: _____

ADJECTIVE: _____

ADJECTIVE: _____

PLURAL NOUN: _____

NUMBER: _____

NOUN: _____

NOUN: _____

PLURAL NOUN: _____

NOUN: _____

NOUN: _____

ADJECTIVE: _____

NOUN: _____

ADJECTIVE: _____

ADJECTIVE: _____

NOUN: _____

ADJECTIVE: _____

NOUN: _____

BOWLING

Bowling is a game in which a/an _____ ball is rolled
ADJECTIVE

along a/an _____ lane in an attempt to knock over
ADJECTIVE

_____ wooden _____. If you
ADJECTIVE   PLURAL NOUN

knock over all _____ pins with your first _____ ,
NUMBER   NOUN

you have made a/an _____. If it takes two balls to
NOUN

knock down all the _____ , you've scored
PLURAL NOUN

a/an _____. If you ever bowl 300, which is the
NOUN

perfect _____, you can expect to be interviewed
NOUN

by _____ sports writers and have your
ADJECTIVE

_____ in the _____ newspaper.
NOUN   ADJECTIVE

Bowling is _____ fun for every member of your
ADJECTIVE

_____ and it is also _____
NOUN   ADJECTIVE

exercise for developing your _____.
NOUN

From *SLAM DUNK MAD LIBS* ® ● Copyright © 1994 by Price Stern Sloan, Inc.

A member of The Putnam & Grosset Group, New York, New York.

MAD LIBS® is fun to play with friends, but you can also play it by yourself! To begin with, DO NOT look at the story on the page below. Fill in the blanks on this page with the words called for. Then, using the words you've selected, fill in the blank spaces in the story.

Now you've created your own hilarious MAD LIB!

AND NOW A WORD FROM...

ADJECTIVE: _____

ADJECTIVE: _____

NOUN: _____

PLURAL NOUN: _____

VERB: _____

ADJECTIVE: _____

PART OF BODY (PLURAL): _____

PLURAL NOUN: _____

ADJECTIVE: _____

ADJECTIVE: _____

NOUN: _____

PART OF BODY: _____

VERB (ENDING IN "ING"): _____

PLURAL NOUN: _____

AND NOW A WORD FROM...

It is almost impossible to watch _____ time
                                      ADJECTIVE

television without having some _____ athlete
                                      ADJECTIVE

pitching a/an _____ for you to buy. They sell you
                  NOUN

everything from soup to_____. They are
                              PLURAL NOUN

spokespersons for sneakers that _____, as well as
                                      VERB

_____ smelling deodorants you put under your
      ADJECTIVE

_____. Other products they endorse
PART OF BODY (PLURAL)

are designer_____, watches with
                  PLURAL NOUN

_____ movements and _____
      ADJECTIVE   ADJECTIVE

razors which they guarantee will remove every_____
                                                      NOUN

from your_____. Athletes make more money
            PART OF BODY

from _____ products than they can
      VERB (ENDING IN "ING")

earn from playing _____.
                        PLURAL NOUN

MAD LIBS® is fun to play with friends, but you can also play it by yourself! To begin with, DO NOT look at the story on the page below. Fill in the blanks on this page with the words called for. Then, using the words you've selected, fill in the blank spaces in the story.

Now you've created your own hilarious MAD LIB!

BASKETBALL INTERVIEW

NAME OF GIRL IN ROOM: _____

NAME OF BOY IN ROOM: _____

NUMBER: _____

NOUN: _____

PLURAL NOUN: _____

ADJECTIVE: _____

NAME OF PERSON IN ROOM: _____

ADJECTIVE: _____

PART OF BODY: _____

PLURAL NOUN: _____

PLURAL NOUN: _____

PLURAL NOUN: _____

NOUN: _____

VERB (ENDING IN "ING"): _____

ADJECTIVE: _____

VERB (PRESENT TENSE): _____

NUMBER: _____

PLURAL NOUN: _____

NOUN: _____

BASKETBALL INTERVIEW

To be read by _____ and
NAME OF GIRL IN ROOM

_____.
NAME OF BOY IN ROOM

QUESTION: Now that you finally signed a/an _____
NUMBER

year _____ with the Miami _____,
NOUN   PLURAL NOUN

how do you feel?

ANSWER: As I said to my _____ friend,
ADJECTIVE

_____, it's a/an _____
NAME OF PERSON IN ROOM   ADJECTIVE

load off my _____.
PART OF BODY

QUESTION: Are you concerned about being able to replace one of

basketball's super_____?
PLURAL NOUN

ANSWER: I only hope I can fill his _____ .
PLURAL NOUN

QUESTION: You set a record for scoring the most

_____ in a single college _____.
PLURAL NOUN   NOUN

Do you think you'll have any trouble

_____ in the pros?
VERB (ENDING IN "ING")

ANSWER: My coach says that with my _____
ADJECTIVE

speed and my ability to slam-_____
VERB (PRESENT TENSE)

that I should score at least _____
NUMBER

_____ a game. I only hope he's in his right
PLURAL NOUN

_____.
NOUN

From *SLAM DUNK MAD LIBS* ® ● Copyright © 1994 by Price Stern Sloan, Inc.

A member of The Putnam & Grosset Group, New York, New York.

MAD LIBS® is fun to play with friends, but you can also play it by yourself! To begin with, DO NOT look at the story on the page below. Fill in the blanks on this page with the words called for. Then, using the words you've selected, fill in the blank spaces in the story.

Now you've created your own hilarious MAD LIB!

THE LITTLE LEAGUERS

PLURAL NOUN: _____

ADJECTIVE: _____

PLURAL NOUN: _____

VERB (PRESENT TENSE): _____

NOUN: _____

PLURAL NOUN: _____

NOUN: _____

PLURAL NOUN: _____

NUMBER: _____

ADJECTIVE: _____

PLURAL NOUN: _____

ADJECTIVE: _____

VERB (PRESENT TENSE): _____

NOUN: _____

THE LITTLE LEAGUERS

Many of today's famous _____ got their start
PLURAL NOUN

playing _____ League baseball. According to the
ADJECTIVE

Guiness Book of _____, Little League baseball
PLURAL NOUN

got its _____ in Williamsport, a small
VERB (PRESENT TENSE)

_____ in Pennsylvania. Today there are Little League
NOUN

_____ in all four corners of the
PLURAL NOUN

_____. Both boys and _____ from
NOUN PLURAL NOUN

the age of 8 to _____ can join the league. Every year
NUMBER

thousands of _____ parents volunteer to instruct
ADJECTIVE

_____ on the rules of the game as well as how
PLURAL NOUN

to practice _____ sportsmanship. One of Little
ADJECTIVE

League's best known slogans is—"It isn't whether you win or

_____ but how you play the _____."
VERB (PRESENT TENSE) NOUN

MAD LIBS® is fun to play with friends, but you can also play it by yourself! To begin with, DO NOT look at the story on the page below. Fill in the blanks on this page with the words called for. Then, using the words you've selected, fill in the blank spaces in the story.

Now you've created your own hilarious MAD LIB!

WOMEN IN SPORTS

PLURAL NOUN: _____

PLURAL NOUN: _____

ADJECTIVE: _____

NOUN: _____

NOUN: _____

VERB (ENDING IN "ING"): _____

ADJECTIVE: _____

ADJECTIVE: _____

VERB (ENDING IN "ING"): _____

ADJECTIVE: _____

NOUN: _____

ADJECTIVE: _____

PLURAL NOUN: _____

WOMEN IN SPORTS

At one time, only men were allowed to play such sports as

_____ and _____ . Today
_{PLURAL NOUN} ... PLURAL NOUN

women athletes have broken that _____ barrier.
ADJECTIVE

Women excel in such track and field events as the 100-yard

_____ , the broad _____ , and even long
NOUN ... NOUN

distance _____ . People love to watch
VERB (ENDING IN "ING")

women win _____ medals in such Olympic
ADJECTIVE

events as _____ gymnastics, figure _____
ADJECTIVE ... VERB (ENDING IN "ING")

and _____ style swimming. Today, there are as many
ADJECTIVE

women as men who listen to the roar of the _____ as
NOUN

they cross the _____ line. Women athletes have
ADJECTIVE

indeed become household _____ .
PLURAL NOUN

MAD LIBS® is fun to play with friends, but you can also play it by yourself! To begin with, DO NOT look at the story on the page below. Fill in the blanks on this page with the words called for. Then, using the words you've selected, fill in the blank spaces in the story.

Now you've created your own hilarious MAD LIB!

TENNIS, ANYONE?

ADJECTIVE: _____

PLURAL NOUN: _____

ADJECTIVE: _____

ADJECTIVE: _____

NOUN: _____

NOUN: _____

VERB (PRESENT TENSE): _____

ADJECTIVE: _____

PART OF BODY: _____

PART OF BODY: _____

NOUN: _____

NOUN: _____

TENNIS, ANYONE?

These days, almost everyone is playing tennis. Young people, middle

_____people and even elderly_____
    ADJECTIVE   PLURAL NOUN

are on the court. Tennis is healthful. It gets you out in the

_____air and is_____exercise.
    ADJECTIVE   ADJECTIVE

The most important part of a good tennis game is the serve. To

serve, you throw the_____ high in the air and hit it
                                   NOUN

into your opponent's _____. Then, you run up to the
                                   NOUN

net and_____the ball with a powerful
                 VERB (PRESENT TENSE)

_____ smash. To master the game, you have to
    ADJECTIVE

have a good fore- _____and an equally good
                     PART OF BODY

back- _____. And most important, if you win a
        PART OF BODY

game, you must always remember to jump over the

_____ and shake your opponent's _____.
    NOUN   NOUN

From *SLAM DUNK MAD LIBS* ® ● Copyright © 1994 by Price Stern Sloan, Inc.

A member of The Putnam & Grosset Group, New York, New York.

MAD LIBS® is fun to play with friends, but you can also play it by yourself! To begin with, DO NOT look at the story on the page below. Fill in the blanks on this page with the words called for. Then, using the words you've selected, fill in the blank spaces in the story.

Now you've created your own hilarious MAD LIB!

WHO IS HE?

NOUN: _____

NOUN: _____

ADJECTIVE: _____

ADJECTIVE: _____

ADJECTIVE: _____

VERB (PRESENT TENSE): _____

ADJECTIVE: _____

PLURAL NOUN: _____

PART OF BODY (PLURAL): _____

ADVERB: _____

PLURAL NOUN: _____

VERB (ENDING IN "ING"): _____

ADJECTIVE: _____

PLURAL NOUN: _____

NAME OF PERSON IN ROOM: _____

NOUN: _____

WHO IS HE?

He always has a/an _____ on his face. He never loses his
                          NOUN

_____. He never argues if a/an _____
        NOUN   ADJECTIVE

decision is made by a/an _____ referee. He is
                                  ADJECTIVE

always in _____ physical shape and does 100
                  ADJECTIVE

_____-ups each and every morning. He
  VERB (PRESENT TENSE)

always has a/an_____word for his teammates and
                    ADJECTIVE

encourages them by slapping them on their_____
                                              PLURAL NOUN

and shaking their_____. He doesn't
                      PART OF BODY (PLURAL)

brag _____, preferring his basketball
              ADVERB

_____to do his_____.
  PLURAL NOUN   VERB (ENDING IN "ING")

Sports writers have called him the most _____
                                                    ADJECTIVE

player to ever put on basketball _____.
                                      PLURAL NOUN

Who is he? He is _____, the most
                      NAME OF PERSON IN ROOM

famous _____ in the world.
            NOUN

From *SLAM DUNK MAD LIBS* ® ● Copyright © 1994 by Price Stern Sloan, Inc.
A member of The Putnam & Grosset Group, New York, New York.

MAD LIBS® is fun to play with friends, but you can also play it by yourself! To begin with, DO NOT look at the story on the page below. Fill in the blanks on this page with the words called for. Then, using the words you've selected, fill in the blank spaces in the story.

Now you've created your own hilarious MAD LIB!

WRESTLING

ADJECTIVE: _____

ADJECTIVE: _____

PART OF BODY: _____

PLURAL NOUN: _____

PLURAL NOUN: _____

ADJECTIVE: _____

PART OF BODY (PLURAL): _____

NOUN: _____

PLURAL NOUN: _____

ADJECTIVE: _____

NOUN: _____

ADJECTIVE: _____

NOUN: _____

ADJECTIVE: _____

PLURAL NOUN: _____

WRESTLING

Wrestling was a/an _____ sport among the
ADJECTIVE

_____ Greeks. Wrestlers were naked to the
ADJECTIVE

_____ and wore _____
PART OF BODY   PLURAL NOUN

around their waists. Wrestlers on television are more

actors than they are _____. They wear
PLURAL NOUN

_____ costumes and pretend to gouge each other's
ADJECTIVE

_____ out, kick each other in the
PART OF BODY (PLURAL)

_____ and jump on each other's _____.
NOUN   PLURAL NOUN

Television wrestlers answer to such _____
ADJECTIVE

names as the Masked _____, the _____
NOUN   ADJECTIVE

Monster from Outer _____ and _____
NOUN   ADJECTIVE

Hogan. Television wrestling is very popular with men and women as

well as teenage _____.
PLURAL NOUN

MAD LIBS® is fun to play with friends, but you can also play it by yourself! To begin with, DO NOT look at the story on the page below. Fill in the blanks on this page with the words called for. Then, using the words you've selected, fill in the blank spaces in the story.

Now you've created your own hilarious MAD LIB!

SCUBA DIVING

FIVE LETTERS OF THE ALPHABET:_____

PLURAL NOUN: _____

PLURAL NOUN: _____

PART OF BODY:_____

PART OF BODY:_____

ADJECTIVE: _____

VERB (PRESENT TENSE): _____

NOUN:_____

PLURAL NOUN: _____

PLURAL NOUN: _____

A LIQUID: _____

PLURAL NOUN: _____

NOUN:_____

SCUBA DIVING

The word "scuba," which is spelled _____ means

"Self-Contained Underwater Breathing _____."

PLURAL NOUN

A scuba diver wears a tank filled with _____

PLURAL NOUN

strapped on his/her_____ and a mask over

PART OF BODY

his/her_____. Divers must be in

PART OF BODY

_____ physical condition to

ADJECTIVE

_____ under water. Warning! Scuba

VERB (PRESENT TENSE)

diving can be a very dangerous_____. Divers may run

NOUN

into man-eating _____ or poisonous

PLURAL NOUN

_____ when they are under the

PLURAL NOUN

_____. Over the years, scuba divers have discovered

A LIQUID

many sunken _____ which have often turned

PLURAL NOUN

out to be worth a small _____.

NOUN

MAD LIBS® is fun to play with friends, but you can also play it by yourself! To begin with, DO NOT look at the story on the page below. Fill in the blanks on this page with the words called for. Then, using the words you've selected, fill in the blank spaces in the story.

Now you've created your own hilarious MAD LIB!

BOXING

ADJECTIVE: _____

PLURAL NOUN: _____

NOUN: _____

ADJECTIVE: _____

ADJECTIVE: _____

NOUN: _____

ADJECTIVE: _____

NOUN: _____

PLURAL NOUN: _____

VERB (ENDING IN "ING"): _____

NOUN: _____

PART OF BODY (PLURAL) : _____

ADJECTIVE: _____

ADJECTIVE: _____

ADJECTIVE: _____

NOUN: _____

BOXING

Television has brought back boxing as a/an _____
ADJECTIVE

attraction. A boxer wears leather _____ on his/her
PLURAL NOUN

hands and a mouthpiece in his/her _____. If you
NOUN

want to be a/an _____ boxer you must have
ADJECTIVE

_____ reflexes and an ability to take a punch in
ADJECTIVE

the _____. To keep in _____
NOUN   ADJECTIVE

condition, boxers train by punching a _____, lifting
NOUN

_____ or _____ a
PLURAL NOUN   VERB (ENDING IN "ING")

rope. All boxers do road-_____ to keep their
NOUN

_____ in _____ shape.
PART OF BODY (PLURAL)   ADJECTIVE

Unfortunately most boxers end up with _____
ADJECTIVE

ears, _____ noses and very little money in the
ADJECTIVE

_____.
NOUN

MAD LIBS® is fun to play with friends, but you can also play it by yourself! To begin with, DO NOT look at the story on the page below. Fill in the blanks on this page with the words called for. Then, using the words you've selected, fill in the blank spaces in the story.

Now you've created your own hilarious MAD LIB!

HOCKEY MAYHEM

PLURAL NOUN: _____

PLURAL NOUN: _____

NOUN: _____

NOUN: _____

ADJECTIVE: _____

NUMBER: _____

NOUN: _____

PLURAL NOUN: _____

ADJECTIVE: _____

NAME OF PERSON IN ROOM: _____

NOUN: _____

NOUN: _____

NOUN: _____

PLURAL NOUN: _____

PLURAL NOUN: _____

ADJECTIVE: _____

ADJECTIVE: _____

PLURAL NOUN: _____

HOCKEY MAYHEM

It definitely wasn't a hockey game that took place between

the Chicago _____ and the New York
                PLURAL NOUN

_____ last night at Madison Square
     PLURAL NOUN

_____. It was more of a wrestling _____
  NOUN   NOUN

or a/an _____ fight. Maybe it was World War
       ADJECTIVE

_____. Five players were sent to the
  NUMBER

_____ with broken _____ and
  NOUN   PLURAL NOUN

_____ eyes. _____
  ADJECTIVE   NAME OF PERSON IN ROOM

who scored the winning _____, was hit in the
                    NOUN

_____ by a hockey _____ and lost all
  NOUN   NOUN

his/her _____. All in all, sixteen _____
      PLURAL NOUN   PLURAL NOUN

were sent to the _____ box. Many fans said it was
              ADJECTIVE

the most _____ game they had ever seen in
          ADJECTIVE

their _____.
    PLURAL NOUN

MAD LIBS® is fun to play with friends, but you can also play it by yourself! To begin with, DO NOT look at the story on the page below. Fill in the blanks on this page with the words called for. Then, using the words you've selected, fill in the blank spaces in the story.

Now you've created your own hilarious MAD LIB!

GOLF

A SOUND: _____

NOUN: _____

NOUN: _____

ADJECTIVE: _____

NOUN: _____

NOUN: _____

PLURAL NOUN: _____

NOUN: _____

A LIQUID: _____

PLURAL NOUN: _____

NOUN: _____

NOUN: _____

ADVERB: _____

PART OF BODY: _____

NOUN: _____

EXCLAMATION: _____

NOUN: _____

GOLF

The word "golf" comes from the German word

"_____" which means club. Golf is an outdoor
    A SOUND

_____ played on a large _____ with a
  NOUN   NOUN

small _____ ball. You use a club with a long,
     ADJECTIVE

slender _____ and a metal or wooden
        NOUN

_____ to hit the ball into a series of eighteen
  NOUN

_____. When you play golf, you try to keep the
   PLURAL NOUN

ball in the middle of the _____, and try to avoid
                                NOUN

_____ hazards and sand _____.
  A LIQUID   PLURAL NOUN

Before you attempt to play golf, you should take lessons from a

professional _____ who will teach you how to swing
          NOUN

your _____ and how to putt _____.
    NOUN   ADVERB

Important: To avoid hitting another player in the

_____ or on top of the_____, be
 PART OF BODY   NOUN

sure to yell _____! This warns them a
           EXCLAMATION

_____ is headed their way.
  NOUN

From *SLAM DUNK MAD LIBS* ® ● Copyright © 1994 by Price Stern Sloan, Inc.
A member of The Putnam & Grosset Group, New York, New York.